CW01430913

Unique Funeral Poems

Dr. Denise Lochrie

DEDICATION

I dedicate this little book of funeral poems to all the beautiful souls who have gone before us…those who have left a legacy of cherished and beautiful memories to hold steadfast in the heart and mind with love   …forevermore.

CONTENTS

.

I share this book with you... with love, light and blessings

Denise *x*

A SYMPHONY OF MUSIC

A Symphony of Music

Is how I'll think of you

A unique composition

That plays your life right through

Encompassing each part of it

From now back to the start

A music touch of specialness

Which captivates my heart

An orchestra of violins

With drums and brass and harps

And every note unlike the next

Diminuendos, crescendos, and sharps

A symphony so beautiful

Imprinted in my heart

To take me through my memories

From me they will never part

And every note will touch a part

Of every thought in mind

Recalling times and memories

They'll not be hard to find

A symphony of music, I dedicate so true

A daughter's/son's/friend's love

To you my dad/mum/friend

Composed from me to you

.

A MESSAGE

I got a message for you today

A word from up above

It's unique and truly wonderful

And sent to you with love

It's filled with joy and laughter

Of hope and peace and love

And surrounded with a heart-felt hug

To keep you nice and snug

The message says you're special

There's no one quite like you

You're simply quite amazing

Completely marvellous too

Now go forth and believe it

And plant it in your heart

And understand that all is well

Although I have to part

A SEED

A seed will grow and flourish

When nurtured everyday

A little drop of water and

The sun beams golden rays

As every petal opens

Letting in the light

Unfolding wonderous beauty

And fragrances in flight

A splash of many colours

To touch each heart and mind

Such beautiful creations

Unique of every kind

And each and every flower

With delicate perfect hues

Will touch my heart perpetually

And remind me so of you

A SWEET LITTLE FLOWER

A sweet little flower

Was sent to us

To nurture with our love

Despite being brief

The time we had

Before you went above

You went to sing with angels

To dance amongst the stars

To play with all the others there

So near and yet so far

We'll love you now and always

Your legacy we'll treasure

Imprinted deep within our hearts and

Impossible to measure

So, our little Angel

We'll leave you to find your way

And look forward to the time when we

Will hold you once again

LILIES AND ROSES

Lilies and roses

A sweet combination

Scented in Heaven

To reach every nation

Coloured with love

Each petal divine

Dusted with silk

All flowers sublime

Lilies and roses

And gerberas too

A splash of green colour

Carnations a few

A bouquet so fine

An expression of love

A mix of sweet flowers

From Heaven above

TWINKLING LIGHT

Whilst searching for an answer

A twinkling light I see

My precious nan/mum/dad/friend

I know that light

Was sent from you to me

To comfort and assure me

That you are always near

To guide me through each moment

With love and without fear

A twinkling light of beauty

A glimmer up above

My lovely nan/mum/dad/friend so special

I send you all my love

AN EXTRA SPECIAL BABY

An extra special baby

Was longed for with our love

But life on earth was not

Meant to be

You were needed far above

You came here for a moment

And love you planted true

With family all united

To say *hello* to you

We'd never have imagined though

That you would have to go

And words cannot express our pain

Because we loved you so

We'll miss you on your birthday

And every day here on…and

We'll think about you always

Our precious little one

CHUBBY CHEEKS AND CUPID'S BOW

Chubby little cheeks and Cupid's bow

Why you had to leave us

Will we ever know?

Longed for with our love

So special from the start

From the moment you were born

We loved you from our hearts

Beautiful little prince/princess

Our earthly prayer come true and

Daily we are grateful

For the time we spent with you

Every waking hour

Of each and everyday

We'll hold you in our memories

By the thoughts and words we'll say

Your legacy is so precious

Our unique and shining star

So cast your light upon us

From the distance near and far

And stay here right beside us

Lighting up the way

Until we too are ready

To meet again one day

EACH AND EVERY MOMENT

Each and every moment

Of every day that's passed

Holds so many memories

And forever they will last

Some of them were perfect

Others falling short

But that's the way that life is

With lessons to be taught

At times we laughed together

We also shed some tears

But we also shared the best times

Over precious long- gone years

So, as we ponder lovingly

And reflect upon the past

We realise how perfect

A precious moment lasts

IF ONLY FOR A MOMENT

If only for a moment

I could have you here with me

I'd tell you that I love you

And what you mean to me

Death robbed us of that instant

When you were set to part and

Although I wasn't beside you

, I held you in my heart

If only at that moment

I could have whispered in your ear

And taken your hand in my own hand

And held you oh so near

So, I'm left with many memories

In this show, stage and time,

A protagonist in the story

, Planned by the Great Divine

A chance to show compassion

A time to love and forgive

To learn from each experience

To appreciate and live

But if only for a moment

I could have you here with me

I'd lead my life so differently

With you right next to me

ILLUMINATING STAR

As I look into the midnight sky

And wonder where you'll be

For deep inside

I know that you're

The brightest star I see

Twinkling in the distance

Beautiful and bright

Illuminating the universe

Shining throughout the night

I sense you're there to show me

That you've found your way

I know you want to let me know

That we'll meet again some day

So, as I stare and wonder

I know within my heart

That this separation's temporary

As we never really part

IT'S NOT THE SAME

It's not the same without you here

As everything stands still

Your special touch

A lonely heart

Which nothing seems to fill

There's a void since you left us

And emptiness and pain

We miss your smile

Your loving words

It will never be the same

We ask, *Why did you leave us?*

Perhaps we'll never know

And all the while we'll wonder why

Our beloved had to go

But special times we'll treasure

And memories we'll hold true

And one thing that's for certain is

We'll never forget you.

LIFE TRULY IS AMAZING

Life truly is amazing

So, appreciate each day

Don't waste your time

Living in the past

And wasting life away

We cannot change the *have beens*

We cannot know *the how's*

But we can live this moment

Appreciating now

Life truly is amazing

Of that there is no doubt

And it's only when our loved ones leave

We know what life's about

Life truly is so special

To live and laugh and love

For all the treasures upon this earth

Can never be enough… so

Appreciate each minute

Of every single day

Live within the moment

And know that, come what may

That each and every person

In every unique way

Has limited time upon this earth

Of years, months and days

Life truly is amazing

Open eyes… and see

Reactivate your senses

And live life's majesty

Life truly is a privilege

A gift of love divine

So, allow the gift, this precious gift

Be thine and thine and thine!

SEEDS OF LOVE

You planted seeds of love

And everyone could see

How special you were dad/mum…

And what you meant to me

Your memory I will cherish

From now right to the end

With every thought embellished

My love, to you I send

Unique and extra special

My dad/mum… you'll always be

And every day I'll think about

Just what you meant to me

No words describe how wonderful

Our memories left behind

My precious mum/dad… forever loved

You'll reign within my heart

NEVER FAR AWAY

Every passing hour

Of each and every day

Memories come to surface

In the mind and heart, they'll stay

With every rising sunset

And dawning of each day

Stars across a night lit sky

You're never far away

A LOVE THAT WAS SO TRUE

When the summer sun feels cooler

And autumn leaves will fall

When winter's round the corner

Your sweet memory I'll recall

The times we shared together

The fun and laughs we had

With love I will remember

The happy and the sad

But most of all I'll cherish

A love that was so true

The legacy of memories

Locked in my heart for you

SMILE AGAIN

Smile again feel joy within

And know I'm always near

With every brand-new day

And turning of each year

Hold each thought and memory

Deep within the heart

For you are me outside of me

A separated part

Smile again feel peace within

Wipe away your tears

Think of all the laughter

We shared throughout the years

There is no need for sadness

There is no need for fear

There is no place for loneliness

For I am always near

THE TIME HAS COME

The time has come

With farewell words

To say a sad goodbye

A multitude of memories

Of love we can't deny

For such is life

We each imprint

A legacy to treasure

Of everything once said and done

Of love we cannot measure

And now we say goodbye to you

And send you on your way

And hope there is a better place

Where we'll meet again someday

YOU WERE VERY SPECIAL TO ME

You were very special to me

My beloved through and through

And every day was a blessing

As I shared my love with you

No matter what life threw us

Through thunders and the rain

The sun- shone through the darkness

And the light would shine again

You were very special to me

My heart I gave to you

And I cherish every moment

Of our love that was so true

YOU'LL REMEMBER ME

You'll remember me today

With a heart that's filled with pain

As you think about our yesterdays

And wish life was the same

You'll remember me tomorrow

Recollecting days gone by

As you comprehend life's brevity

And accept that each must die

You'll remember me every year

As passing seasons fly

As you honour anniversaries

And good times with a sigh

You'll remember me in decades

With tired mind, and soul

And aged body falling weak

As time does take it's toll

You'll remember me and then

Our hands entwined as one

As I lead you to The Promised Land

Past, present, and future as one

You'll remember me and then

You'll remember me and then

You'll remember me and then

Until we meet again

WHAT IF?

What if all that was and is

Is just as it's meant to be?

What if life's ups and downs

With all uncertainties

What if every wrong or right

Forms part of a perfect plan?

And really is a learning curve

For woman, child and man

And what If *this…* that we each see

Within the physical eye

Is merely an illusion

For us to discover why?

So, if you could choose your own life plan

How would it really be?

Would you be happy as you are

Or change your destiny?

What if you with the blink of an eye

Could live a blissful life?

Would you still choose your partner

As your husband lover or wife?

And what if you discovered

That everything is true

And that you hold the key to life

So, it's really down to you

Would you change your mind set?

Would you change your ways?

Would you change your thoughts

In the up and coming days?

Would you treat each other more

With kindness and respect?

Living life an ideal life

With love and no regrets?

So be there for each other

Ride the waves of grief

Remembering that life on earth

Is only very brief

BECAUSE YOU WERE

Because you were my friend

You were a very special treasure

The memories of our yesterdays

Hold happiness and pleasure

Life is very special

And every year that's past is

A legacy locked in my heart

Of years once shared to last

So, I'll cherish every moment

And live and love and be

And hold onto the memories

That you shared with me

MY LOVELY DARLING

My lovey darling sister/brother

I'll miss you beyond measure

I remember you in our childhood days

As my very special treasure

The memories of our yesterdays

When we would dance and sing and play

And we'd talk about what we would do

When all grown up one day

Life holds many legacies

The key is held in the mind

And a sister/brother such as you

Is so very hard to find

LIFE'S LESSONS

Appreciate the past

Don't plan too much ahead

Live this very moment

Life without a dread

Bring loving memories forward

Take heed of words you say

Filter thoughts and actions

Meditate and pray

Appreciate all seasons

Don't curse the blessed rain

Keep your body healthy

Ride the waves of pain

Focus on the good things

Live and laugh and learn

Love they neighbour as yourself

Be attentive and discern

So, love the life you're living

As it passes all too fast

Hold a treasure chest of memories

In the heart and mind to last

NEVER FAR APART

Although the heart feels heavy now

Don't let it stay that way

Remember all the good times

And… think of those today

Remember first encounters

With loved ones very dear

Remember happy times with joy

Don't think about the tears

Reflect on all the memories

Hold onto something real

Think of all the special times

No one, can ever steal

And so, I'm on my way now

To pave the way and see

As you continue on your path

Unfolding destiny

Remember all the best times

And hold peace in your heart

And know I'm always near you

As from you I'll never part

WILL I GET TO HEAVEN

Will I get to heaven?

I'll have to wait and see

Until I'm called

I'll live my life with some uncertainty

Will I sing with angels?

And explore the moon lit stars?

Be pardoned for my errors?

And discover planets from afar?

Will I get to meet God?

Will he know my name?

And will he understand that I

Was not always to blame?

But for now, I'm rather happy

Living in this skin

And won't be bothered with earthly rules

And all that stuff called *sin*

For as long as I live fully

With love and faith and hope

And offer my compassion

To all the other folk

And, as long as I am conscious

I'll be the best that I can be and

I'm sure, that there'll be one more place

In eternity for me!

AN AVID FOOTBALL FAN

I loved to watch the football

It was my favourite game and

Every match unlike the last

They never were the same

The crowds all cheered together

(name of team) we love you!

Waving scarves and banners

And even singing too

An avid fan of footy

I loved to watch them play

So, continue on without me

Supporting come what may

And, I'll keep up tradition

No matter where I'll be

Cheering on behind the veil

Of course, you won't spot me

But rest assured I'll be there

My team within my heart

A little space between us

Doesn't mean were far apart

So, remember when your cheering

That I am cheering too

Of course, supporting ……….

My favourite team so true!

ON DAYS LIKE THESE

On days like these thoughts flood to mind

Of things once said and done

Including all the happy times

Good memories and the fun

The joy once shared together

The laughter, sometimes pain

Events and anniversaries

The sunshine and the rain

On days like these, reflective times

Emotions real and true

A heavy heart a fleeting thought

A mind so full of you

And sadness overwhelming

Fighting back the tears

Trying hard to look so brave

Despite compounding fear

On days like these

One really feels the magnitude of grief

A mindful of… *if onlys*

Always there to keep

So, to ease the loss and sadness

I'll focus on the best

Knowing that there's no more pain

And leave you now to rest

DRY AWAY THOSE TEARS

Put away your handkerchiefs

Dry away those tears

Remember all the fun and joy

We shared over the years

Put away your sadness

Lock away the fears

Remember all the greatest times

And celebrate those years

Call my name and love me

For I am simply me

I've merely followed a chartered course

And followed my destiny

So, wipe away your tears now

Love me come what may

And know that when the time is right

We'll meet again some day

CROSSROADS OF MY LIFE

At the crossroads of my life

I chose an alternate path

I passed right through the sacred veil

And left all aftermath

I know that there is heartache

For that I can't deny

And many unanswered questions

And lots of tears to cry

I feel your heart is breaking

I'm sorry for the pain

But I also know that it's not the end

As in time, we'll meet again

I was guided by an angel

Who took me through the light

A splendid wonderous feeling

No worries, pain or fight

And now I'll wait with patience

As you journey on alone

And look forward to our encounter

The day when you come home

BRIGHT LIT STAR ABOVE

Once upon a star lit sky

A gateway straight to Heaven

Angels guarded and kept close watch

Of realms they call *The Seven*…

And as they always did back then

They continue even now

Lovingly and protective

Whispering and guiding how

Silently invisible, to the naked eye

But always near

To off- set harm

Whenever harm appears

There are many secret portals

In this universe

To guide the many mortals

And help them to traverse

And everything you see

With the naked eye

Is not always as it seems

And we're left to wonder why

And with a pre- planned mission

To experience life on earth

A destined time to accomplish

Which ticks away from birth

And some can glimpse into it

Before they pass away

And see things oh so clearly

In every single way

And others never awaken

To secrets far and true

And live their lives so busily

With many things to do

So, when you have a doubt in mind

Of all there was and is

Remember there's a reason

For every soul that lives

It's merely to accomplish

Experience and love

Before returning, to that place

To the bright lit star above

A SIMPLE ACT OF KINDNESS

A simple act of kindness

Beyond what eyes can see

Can touch the heart profoundly

The price of which is free

A simple word or gesture

Can change a person's day

And elevate emotions

Such a tiny price to pay

A simple caring moment

Compassion at its best

Shows love and understanding

A consciousness at rest

A simple act of kindness

A gesture plain and sweet

An errand, shoulder or a cup of tea

A favour or a treat

And all the things just mentioned

Are not so hard to do

Sometimes, a simple phone-call

To say, *Thinking of You*

So next time when you're busy

Wrapped up in your own ways

Just take a slice of goodness

And change somebody's day!

RIDE THE WAVES

Ride the waves of sadness

Wipe away the tears

Don't hesitate the laughter

We shared across the years

This separation's temporary

It's only set to be

A twinkle in the star lit sky

In all eternity

So, celebrate your lives now

Make the most of every day

Live each precious moment

And love life come what may

Do everything you've dreamed of

Love life come what may
And then tell me all about it
When we meet again some day

ABOUT THE AUTHOR

My name is Denise Lochrie and I was born in Saltburn by the Sea on the North East Coast of England in the U.K.

As a child, I had always dreamed of becoming a Midwife and was also fascinated with learning another language and I'm pleased to say, that over time, I was able to accomplish both.

Following almost ten years of living in Sicily/Italy, I returned to the U.K. with my young daughter Nathalie-Jean. I subsequently attended college and worked hard in order to pass the qualifications to get a place at university.

In 1998, after four years studying for a degree at the University of Greenwich in London, I obtained a BSc (Hons) in Midwifery. I loved this role very much and felt deeply privileged to have been part of such a wonderful and special time in families' lives. The wealth of experience gained over those years, will stay with me always.

Over the course of time, I have continued to study and achieved various other qualifications - including a Diploma in Events & Wedding Planning and a Doctorate in Metaphysical Hypnosis - but an equally special role, is my current position as an Independent Celebrant (Funerals and Weddings).

I feel very honoured to be - and have been - part of significant and important events in life… from birth to death, and am without doubt, very privileged in my current role as a Celebrant.

I hope that my simple verses bring a degree of comfort to those who are grieving and can offer a little help during sad, difficult and challenging experiences in life.

Printed in Great Britain
by Amazon